housebeautiful Art

DECORATING WITH ART AT HOME

The Editors of House Beautiful Magazine

Text by

JUDITH GURA

HEARST BOOKS ● NEW YORK

Library of Congress Cataloging-in-Publication Data

House beautiful art : decorating with art at home /
Judith Gura and the editors of House beautiful.
p. cm.
ISBN 1-58816-023-8
1. Art in interior decoration. I. Gura, Judith. II. House beautiful.
nk2115.5.A77 H678 2001
747--dc21   2001024514

Printed in China

FIRST EDITION

1   2   3   4   5   6   7   8   9   10

Edited by Laurie Orseck
Designed by Susi Oberhelman

PRODUCED BY SMALLWOOD & STEWART, INC., NEW YORK, NY

www.housebeautiful.com

Contents

Introduction

WHETHER WE REALIZE IT OR NOT, MOST OF US EXPERIENCE art every day. Beyond the walls of galleries and museums, it permeates our lives—in the workplace, in restaurants and shops, theaters and sports arenas, even on the streets of our cities and towns. But the art we take into our homes engages us more intimately than anything in the world outside. The objects we own may be old or new, priceless or inexpensive, flat or three-dimensional, of almost any size, material, or composition. We may arrange them meticulously, or scatter them haphazardly around a room. The ways in which we live with art are matters of individual choice, but the fact that so many of us choose to do so says much about its value in enriching our lives—and perhaps affirming our humanity.

Since prehistoric men painted images on the walls of caves, humans have created some sort of art to adorn their surroundings. Medieval priests and prelates commissioned it for cathedrals, monarchs for their palaces. Renaissance scholars assembled "cabinets of curiosities" for private study, and eighteenth-century Englishmen collected it to show their cultivated taste.

By the nineteenth century, with the opening of public museums, more people had the opportunity to appreciate art—and to own it. In time, collecting became the practice of many rather than an elite few. The pursuit of connoisseurship propels the search for wonderful things to admire and, with good fortune, to possess. The author Vladimir Nabokov once observed, "A work of art has no importance whatever to society. It is only important to the individual." In this book we've visited homes whose interiors reflect that importance to the people who inhabit them. The objects are very different in period, style, size, and composition. Some are priceless and some plebian, yet all are equally valued by their owners. And the homes themselves are as varied as the collections they contain.

"Art isn't easy," composer Steven Sondheim has written. Indeed it isn't—not easy to create, and often not easy to understand. Fortunately, however, it can be easy to live with, as the homes on these pages prove.

Inspiratio

The owners whose homes are profiled on the following pages collect art out of passion and personal artistic vision. The rooms they live in were designed to give their collections pride of place. These interiors are highly individualistic, even eccentric, and they may not appeal to everyone—nor are they intended to. They were planned to make art an integral part of the design, permeating the very life of the home. In this, each of them achieves an absolute purity.

Victorian with Verve

All Victorian charm on the outside, this Connecticut cottage is winningly this-minute modern inside its painted doors. The occupants, a couple who have been collecting art for almost three decades, bought the 1886 house with their art in mind, knowing that its spacious, high-ceilinged rooms would provide the right backgrounds for the broad selection of contemporary pieces. From the beginning, they bought only what they loved rather than what was fashionable or critically acclaimed. The collection incorporates large paintings and more modest-size graphics by a number of modern masters, as well a variety of works by lesser-known artists that appealed to their sharp eyes and eclectic good taste. Far from competing with the art, the balanced proportions of the rooms and the architectural detailing of moldings, window frames, and mantels provide a graceful framework to highlight its best features. An initial bright palette for the walls was muted to a monochromatic scheme that brings the objects into sharp relief. Most of the works are relatively small, so they could be hung in close proximity without creating a cluttered environment and without having any single piece overwhelm a room.

The lady of the house, a passionate amateur decorator, has a penchant for unlikely partnerships and unusual juxtapositions. The offhandedness of the

Almost every corner holds a pleasant surprise. On a console table in a hallway, above, a Matisse portrait sits on an easel below a pair of Bryan Hunt drawings. Just outside the parlor, opposite, the oarlock from a gondola makes a surprisingly elegant sculpture to underscore a Philip Guston drawing. In the living room beyond, several moods and media are represented, including a ladderlike sculpture by Bruce Robbins and, on the mantel, a section of a nineteenth-century iron fence beneath a Susan Rothenberg drawing.

arrangements, however, is illusory. Though they appear to be placed in random and sometimes unrelated groupings, the objects are continually moved around by the owners in an effort to create new and fresh viewing angles. The result of these frequent rearrangements, in addition to keeping boredom at bay, are unpretentious, appealing, and very livable interiors that offer a constant series of delights for the eye.

The inviting air of the back parlor, above, comes from a carefully crafted blend of not-quite-old and not-blatantly-new. To the left of the windows is a Richard Diebenkorn drawing; an Alexander Calder mobile swings between painted topiaries and nineteenth-century fence finials. An extravagant Empire sofa holds court in the front parlor, right; above it is a set of Victorian shoe prints that step smartly in the space between bare windows. In an unexpected pairing, the John Duff sculpture on the wall at left echoes the silhouette of the Isamu Noguchi lamp in the opposite corner. A lively orange wood sculpture on the coffee table keeps the subtle color scheme from becoming dull.

The offbeat mix
of paintings and objects continues
in the dining room, opposite, with Lois
Lane's mixed-media framed artwork
hung over a shelf arranged with
clusters of Sheffield candlesticks and a
Chinese export porcelain bowl. The
bedroom gets its energy from a
palette of black and white: above right,
a bold painting by Roger Brown
opposite the bed, a charcoal drawing
and iron ornaments over the mantel;
below right, a strong Susan Rothenberg
oil over the bed, a Katherine Porter
drawing on the wall, and a Stuart Shils
drawing on the end table.

Milanese Mélange

The beautiful proportions of this
fifteenth-century Milanese palazzo bespeak its aristocratic
lineage, but the mix of centuries and periods within its walls
bears the stamp of the owner's distinctive personal style. As a
child, designer Piero Castellini Baldissera played in the
antiques-filled interiors of the Casa degli Atellani, then the
home of his grandfather, the celebrated architect Piero
Portaluppi. Across from the church of Santa Maria delle
Grazie, where Leonardo da Vinci painted *The Last Supper*—
and which Portaluppi restored—the palazzo was filled with
the fruits of its owner's insatiable penchant for collecting.
From his illustrious ancestor, Baldissera inherited both
impeccable taste and a similar desire to acquire beautiful
things. In 1985, he fulfilled a lifelong dream by reclaiming
his grandfather's apartment in the palazzo from fashion
designer Valentino, who as an interim tenant had used it as
his couture showroom.

Restoring parts of the interior and improvising
others—a tented ceiling for the winter-garden foyer and
a faux-coffered vaulted one in a salon, for example—
Baldissera filled the gloriously proportioned rooms with
treasures acquired in his extensive travels: such intriguing
oddities as pieces of coral, antique fabrics, and dozens of
medallions picturing emperors and popes (attracted to an
object, Baldissera is apt to acquire it in multiples). Rather

In the winter-garden foyer,
the designer has created a blend of fine art and illusion. An
explosion of real and imaginary foliage wraps the room in an
enveloping trompe l'oeil overgrowth. Between the arched
doorways, an Empire settee once owned by Napoleon's sister is
almost buried beneath art books. Behind it, a Louis XVI screen,
its fabric cover removed, is topped with gilt arrowhead finials.

than being meticulously placed, the art is scattered around the rooms, arranged in an abandoned mix of periods and sources. This offhand élan keeps the combination of landmark building and classical objects from being intimidating. Balancing respect for the objects with occasional touches of whimsy, Baldissera's interiors have an air of contemporary informality, without the slightest hint of mustiness or age.

Dominating one of the dining rooms, opposite, a massive Louis XV limestone fireplace makes a major architectural statement. The frescoes that flank it, once threatened with destruction, were moved by Baldissera's grandfather from the palazzo facade to their present spot. In a crowded tablescape, above left, Roman busts and classical obelisks are paired beneath a balanced wall grouping; in the foyer behind it, Baldissera devised a coffered classical ceiling that seems to have always been part of the house. In the library, above right, samples of antique marble line the bookcase shelves in a new take on Renaissance *pietra dura*.

Crafted to Perfection

If every work of art in this grand-scaled duplex apartment in Manhattan seems to have been made for the space it occupies, that's because it probably was. The owners are a crafts-collecting couple; the wife a former chairman of the American Crafts Council. Wishing to make their new quarters a showplace for contemporary craft art, and knowing where to find the artists whose work she most admired, she offered them the challenge of

Brilliant geometry in the entry hall, above left, is introduced by Jean Dunand's red-and-silver lacquer panels from the 1925 Paris Exposition, mounted above an angular table of scoured stainless steel. Drawing the visitors into the space, above right, is a zigzag rug by Elizabeth Browning Jackson. In the garden room, right, each object has its place: the assertive Sandro Chia painting on its own divider wall; the metal console by André Dubreuil beneath a raffia hanging, proportioned perfectly to fit its space. Whimsical raffia-skirt stools by Elizabeth Garouste and Mattia Bonetti break up the space, and contemporary art ceramics are on display against a rear wall.

creating objects of their own choice to suit particular locations within the apartment. The result is an extraordinary residence, planned with intelligence and a focused point of view. It is a spectacular presentation of artworks, but one that replaces the impersonality of a gallery with a warm and welcoming air. From the entry hall, a sequence of three conjoined spaces establishes continuous sight lines from the entry through the living room to the garden room. Furnished with overscale seating, its backgrounds are almost severely simple, allowing the objects to take over. The fact that so many strong-minded works can coexist comfortably in the same home is the result of meticulous planning: Not only their specific locations but the color schemes and juxtapositions of objects were determined in cooperation with the artisans themselves. Most of the large-scale pieces are displayed individually; others are partnered with complementary works of similar size in noncompeting media. Small-scale art glass and ceramics are housed in specially designed display shelves. Since each object was designed for the space it inhabits, moving a single one would disturb the carefully planned composition. But there is no feeling of stiffness in these interiors; the vitality of the art and the flow of the rooms make this apartment an object lesson in how to present cutting-edge art in a setting that still feels like a home.

Throughout the apartment, the creative craftspeople improvised freely on conventional furniture forms. In the living room, on the black metal fireplace by Bruce McLean, opposite, a graffiti-like face overlooks a pair of Frank Gehry's corrugated stools. A cluster of handcrafted objects sits on the glass-topped table, and a swirl-patterned rug, below right, provides underpinning for a pair of Tom Dixon's twisted-metal see-through female silhouettes, shaped into quirky seating pieces. At the window beyond, African sculptures are silhouetted against the cityscape. Below left, the living room's eye-stopper: a madly Cubistic—and working—grand piano by Fred Baier.

Scribbled faces
on the top and the base of Bruce
McLean's marble dining table
are sisters to the one in the living
room. An acrylic plastic unit
showcases a selection of modern
studio glass by various craftspeople.
The unadorned windows allow
maximum daylight in, flattering the
reflecting surfaces without distracting
from the art objects.

Metropolitan Renaissance

Entering this extraordinary apartment, visitors are transported into another era, one whose Old World ambience belies its New York location. The occupants, owners of an inherited collection of museum-quality furniture and paintings, knew that furnishing a home with such treasures wasn't simply a matter of finding space to fit them.

Every room in the apartment has been transformed into a surrounding worthy of the objects it contains. In the marble-tiled foyer, above left, doors are painted with classical gold-and-white *rinceaux*, and the walls between them hung with Renaissance-style gouaches painted by Mongiardino's artisans. In the elevator vestibule, above right, one of a pair of Neoclassical bas-reliefs by Danish sculptor Bertil Thorvaldsen occupies a stenciled wall. High drama in the library, opposite: Magnificently overscale eighteenth-century Chinese lacquer panels are set into bookcases that wrap around the library, enclosing it in rich color.

The classically detailed rooms were a start, but these Renaissance and Baroque objects demanded interiors of equal splendor. Still, the owners had no desire to turn their home into a stuffy environment weighed down by antiquity.

Enter Renzo Mongiardino, a brilliant Italian designer in the grand tradition, renowned for the sumptuous interiors he created with the eye-fooling skills of a stage designer and a hatful of dazzling special effects. Like the best of Mongiardino's work, these rooms have a classical feel but are not precisely authentic. The designer used simple paint and plaster to infuse the interiors with a sense of the past, giving them a timelessness to match the grandeur of the furnishings and art. Then, to add drama and more than a hint of whimsy, he set a coterie of skilled craftspeople to work on the use of trompe l'oeil as an art form. They created richly colored walls throughout, painted to take on different guises: plasterwork in the foyer, tile in the living room, and foliage in the dining room. The results are infinitely luxurious, with the patina of age on every surface—sometimes real, sometimes deftly re-created. The atmosphere is comfortable rather than stiff, and the owners' furniture and art collections blend seamlessly into this surround. As Mongiardino once said, "I'm not a decorator, I'm a creator of ambience." Indeed he was.

The living room is a total work of art,
a kaleidoscope of hue and pattern, keyed to a rich color scheme of deep jewel tones. The same colors are echoed in a pair of rare Renaissance majolica jugs on top of matched Baroque cabinets behind the sofas. The walls are extravagantly painted in a multicolor geometric pattern that gives the illusion of Venetian tile, forming an enveloping background to flatter the old-master paintings in the room. Underscored by a sixteenth-century rug, seventeenth-century seating combines well with newly designed pieces upholstered in heavy silks and damasks.

A trompe l'oeil mural turns the dining room, above and right, into a fantasy forest clearing. A large round table, seventeenth-century Italian highback chairs, and a Venetian glass chandelier give real-life substance to the setting. On the same grand scale is a pair of massive marble vases on Adam pedestals, balanced by another pair of classical French Empire torchères on caryatid bases on the opposite wall. For a refreshingly witty note in this museum-worthy company, the rug is ordinary sisal, painted with the pattern of a Persian carpet, proving that creating a luxurious look doesn't always demand an extravagant budget.

Soho Meets Santa Fe

On the outside, this L-shaped Santa Fe home fits right in with its low-profile, pink adobe neighbors, but within the walls, it opens into a high-ceilinged expanse that suggests a big-city industrial loft. The owner, lured from New York to the Southwest by a new job, wanted a home that would accommodate her collection of modern art. Finding land on which to build the modern house she envisioned was no problem; placing it in a neighborhood whose dominant design is firmly Southwestern ethnic was the stumbling block. Architect David Lake helped solve the problem by creating an urbane modern

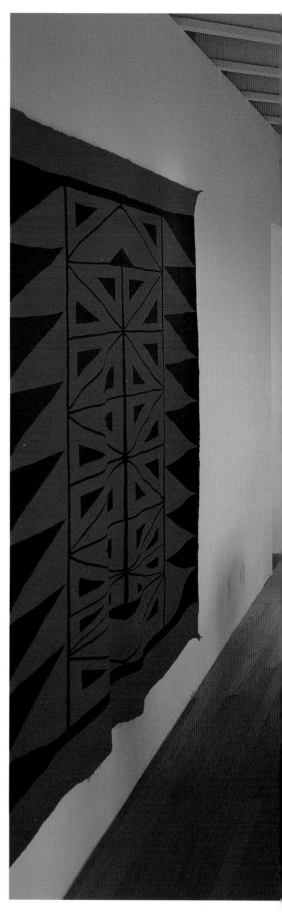

Beyond the front door, a low-ceilinged foyer, above, holds tantalizing hints of the collections beyond: Robert Gil De Montes's *Jaguar*, Cindy Sherman's *Untitled Film Still*, and in a wall niche, a Buddha sculpture. The living room, right, is an expansive, open space, home to two artworks in striking counterpoint: On the white wall, opposite Allan McCollum's *Thirty Plaster Surrogates* of black-and-white shadow-box shapes, is the simplicity of a Navaho rug. Small horizontal windows, set almost at floor level, were devised by the architect as a way to bring in natural light while protecting the art from the harsh desert sun.

environment inside and a neighborhood-friendly exterior: He came up with the ingenious solution of digging down instead of building up.

The new floor plan consists basically of an L-shaped main level intersecting with two lower ones that cross it diagonally. The land had formerly been occupied by a country club, the basement of which provided an already excavated space from which to carve out the lower levels. Lake designed a series of contiguous spaces for the ground-floor library, living room, and bedroom; a staircase leads down to a 17-foot-high gallery reserved for larger artworks, and then to a triangular greenhouse several steps below that. All the floors are joined by a steel-railed bridge that overlooks the gallery. Art is placed throughout the house to make the most of good sight lines. Rather than being grouped, pieces are set apart so they can be viewed one at a time, allowing the eye to take in each as a separate experience.

The lower gallery, left, carved out of the basement of the pre-existing building, is set at angles to the rest of the house in order to align with the best possible light. Its 17-foot ceiling provides space for larger artworks, like the Robert Longo painting at left and the tall geometric by Luis Cruz Azaceta. In muted tones that don't distract from the art, classic Alvar Aalto and Marcel Breuer chairs are grouped comfortably for informal piano recitals. The stairway to the greenhouse a level below adds its complementary geometry to the arrangement. The bedroom, above, is a spare retreat, punctuated only by a photograph by Lorna Simpson and a Picasso owl sculpture.

Plastics Perfect

The owner of this modern high-rise apartment, a New York professional, was living happily with Miesian furniture in International Style interiors until she chanced upon an example of Gaetano Pesce's work. Captivated by the Italian artist-designer's uniquely extroverted vision, she commissioned first one piece and then another, until her modern interiors were subsumed into the exuberant new aesthetic of free-form shapes and brilliant colors. Having discovered a hidden passion for color, she encouraged the designer to create a total environment to accommodate it. The result is an explosion of vibrant hues and imagination, furnished with one-of-a-kind shapes mostly molded from polyester resin.

Pesce has been working with plastics, foams, and resins for more than three decades. He chose polyester resin for this project because of its translucency, warmth to the touch, and ability to take on almost any form and variation of intense color. Throughout the apartment, he installed poured floors in a swirling flow of variegated color,

The living room, opposite, is filled almost entirely with Pesce's designs; the exceptions are the Kenneth Snelson sculpture and a pair of Mies van der Rohe Barcelona chairs, all surprisingly at ease in the provocative setting. The brilliant-blue industrial-looking wall unit, its sail-like projection an unexpected fillip, seems more like sculpture than furniture, but it functions efficiently for storage. In the same room, above, Pesce's much-photographed Sunset Over New York foam sofa and Rag Chair sit on the whimsical resin floor design that takes the place of a conventional rug.

Throughout the apartment, polyester resin takes many guises: above left, as a red coat signaling the hall closet and, above right, as a translucent sleeping man with rainbow-hued dreams marking the entry to the bedroom corridor. Seen through colorful resin doors, opposite left, Pesce's Cannareggio sofa keeps company with an Eames LCW chair and cube tables made of shredded fabric. In the dining room, opposite right, a wall hanging of resin is patterned with an image of the Rag Chair. On the sleek steel-legged table, a many-tentacled vase suggests a fantasy sea creature. The Frank Gehry corrugated-paper chair in the corner, the Isamu Noguchi lamp (its base removed so that it can also be suspended), and the Mies van der Rohe chairs around the table seem conservative by contrast.

punctuated with whimsical images and graphics that reflect the function of each room. The same material was used to form doorways and divider panels as well as decorative pieces such as a skinlike wall hanging. A few remaining remnants of the owner's previous existence, as well as early Pesce foam seating pieces, coexist with surprising ease in the new surroundings. With such a profusion of attractions, no single object stands out, but the interiors as a whole create an invigorating artistic experience. And the consistent presence of humor is a reminder that art doesn't need to be serious to command respect.

GENEROSITÀ?
SPAZIO DELLE
COSE DA
FARE E DA
NON
DIMENTI-
COSE
SPAZIO
PER
MANTENERE
GLI
IMPEGNI
E LE
PROMESSE
FATTE

Greeting guests in the entry foyer, above, is a playful cabinet made of papier-mâché over plywood in a series of irregular shadow-box shapes. On top, an assemblage of unrelated objects forms a collage of abstract shapes, contrasting textures, and interesting materials. In the bedroom, opposite left, an anthropomorphic cabinet wraps the television in a cozy embrace; on the headboard, opposite right, the artist improvised with colored pencils to sketch a face gazing toward the ceiling.

French Accentuated

Choosing to be modern doesn't mean abandoning the past—at least not according to doyenne French designer Michelle Halard. Her undeniably charming Paris home, a work in progress for more than half a century, is perhaps the best example of this all-inclusive philosophy. Irreverently unafraid of mixing contemporary with traditional forms, she is equally adventurous when it comes to color, pattern, and objects. To her, there's nothing that can't be treated as art, and the apartment she shares with her husband, a dedicated toy collector, incorporates everything from theater props and flea-market finds to vintage furniture and assorted artworks of all sizes and periods. Starting

Typical of the casual clutter of this designer's style: On the mantel, above left, is a group of objects that look as though they've been left there en route to a more permanent location—dried flowers, unframed graphics, and a carved bird figure. The funky chair of wood and cardboard, above center, was originally a stage prop. Victorian papered boxes, above right, form an unsettling still life with a pair of doll's arms. Opposite, looking through the enfilade of rooms affords a view, past unmatched and unaligned walls of artworks, all the way to the kitchen, with its own shelves filled with bits and pieces of art.

out with high-ceilinged rooms and a framework of fine architectural moldings, the apartment, in an eighteenth-century building in Paris's sixth arrondissement, has been updated with a sparkling palette of surprising colors that banish the very notion of neutrality and embrace the mix of furnishings. In each of the spaces—the violet dining room, deep green salon, rose bedroom, and mustard-color bath—rare and rustic objects are joined in arrangements that, like the most successful of mixed-media treatments, appear almost accidental rather than meticulously planned. Antique toys are scattered about, pictures are framed and matted in myriad fashion and hung in seemingly random groupings. The apartment is living proof that there is no rule that can't be broken.

The salon, opposite, is another mix of patterns and periods as well as objects. A fine French crystal chandelier sheds ambient light on the wall-to-wall art, most of it modest in both size and provenance. The pieces are casually hung with minimal effort at alignment and only the benefit of Halard's eagle eye to pull them together. Flouting convention in the dining room, above left, violet walls are a strong background for another mélange: multi-colored high-back chairs, an eighteenth-century chandelier intended for outdoor use, and a painted cabinet chock-full of curiosities. The mirror on the wall, above right, is a flea-market find; next to it is an old Gothic-style lantern.

The kitchen, opposite, is a feast for the eyes as well as the appetite. Paintings and graphics in varying styles and subject matter enliven the verdigris-painted walls, and unmatched candlesticks add another homey touch. Warming up things even more is a colorful Moroccan rug. In such an environment, even utensils and storage containers assume the aura of objets d'art. In the small bedroom, above right, the painting of an eighteenth-century lady is an unexpected visitor in a countrified setting of unpretentious furniture and mixed patterns. In the bathroom, below right, rows of antique bottles on the tub surround (designed by Halard) and a collage of family photos give the feeling of a Victorian cottage.

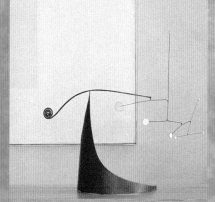

Collections

Looking at beautiful objects is pure pleasure, but owning them is a commitment on many levels. Though we freely enjoy art in many locations, bringing it into the home is like taking responsibility for a living thing. No matter how modest a collection's contents, it demands its own breathing space, appropriate dress, considerate care, and fair share of attention. Outfitting interiors for art isn't always easy, but the rewards are considerable: the joy of living with exquisite things.

The Artful Interior

A COLLECTION IS AS INDIVIDUAL AS A FINGERPRINT. No two art-filled environments, then, follow the same formula. Artworks can dominate a space or be integrated into it, serve as pivot point or be part of the background, shout for attention or whisper into receptive ears. They may be showcased like gems, scattered with abandon, densely clustered, or suspended in space. And like flowers of different species, each blooms in its own nurturing soil. The artful interior is a reflection of individual taste, emotional touchstones, and cultural values, frequently revealing secrets of its occupants' inner lives.

The artful home doesn't usually begin with the search for a painting to hang over a sofa, a sculpture to fill a corner, or a mural to define a color scheme. It's often the end result of our very human impulse to surround ourselves with things that give us pleasure. More likely, it begins with a single piece—a painting, a sketch, a handmade piece of furniture—bought at a local art show, bid on at auction, received as a gift or inheritance. When it is joined by a second, then a third, and so on, the collecting impulse has probably taken root.

How is a series of objects, acquired by choice or by chance, for different reasons or no reason in particular, transformed into a collection? At one moment in the process, a common thread emerges to link one object to another. The owner develops a point of view, a set of criteria, a specific wish for a particular type of work to fit into the blend, and the once random assortment has become a collection, with a life of its own. Its owner has moved from casual pleasure, to serious interest, to the commitment—perhaps the passion—that fuels an ongoing search.

Arranging the fruits of this pursuit at home may appear serendipitous, but it most often takes painstaking planning, a keen eye, and—most important—a defining point of view. The design of such spaces is an art in itself. There is

An arrangement of smallish objects can add up to more than the sum of its parts. A group of framed artworks—and one quirky sculpture—are layered on a low, narrow foyer table, attracting notice that prompts closer examination. Above them, a bold black-and-white painting provides balance to the tablescape.

no single formula for success, but there are some basic guidelines, incorporating the elements of scale, proportion, and balance. Scale, the relative size of objects to the space, determines whether an object or group of objects is dominant or whether the space itself is the focal point. Proportion comes into play in many ways: the relationship of one object to its neighbor, the relationship of the painting to the frame or the sculpture to its pedestal, and the relationship of the art to the furnishings that surround it. Balance refers to the way objects are arranged to effect visual equilibrium; in addition to balance of mass, there are balances of color, materials, form, pattern, and texture to consider.

Though part of any successful interior, these qualities aren't applied in the same way in every case. Conventional practice, for example, calls for grand rooms for housing large artworks—but an overscale piece can be enhanced by a relatively confined area. Similarly, a smallish object, often lost in expansive space,

One work of art or several objects treated as one are often all a room needs. In a refined urban setting, bare-bones color and powerful art are a winning combination. In the dining room, opposite, a single painting is the only element needed to create the Art Deco mood, flattered by spare furnishings that stand in relief against its dynamic lines and moody coloring. The neutral-toned living room, below left, defers to one large-scale but understated framed work that fills the entire wall space over the sofa. In the bedroom, below right, a cluster of wide-matted photographs brings ceiling-stretching height and intensity to a narrow space.

gains stature when massed with similar—or more provocatively, with different—pieces.

The need for symmetry is another guideline that need not be applied in absolute terms. Weight and balance are determined by sensory perception as much as by precise measurements. Meticulously balanced rooms, with every object in perfect alignment, are sometimes more boring than beautiful. A visual balance of multicolored, multitextured, and variously shaped objects can be a more satisfying solution, juxtaposing striking and subtle, textured and smooth, straight-lined and sinuous. An assertive painting on one wall, for example, can be a counterpoint to a substantial cabinet on the opposite one; a tall sculpture might complement an adjacent cluster of more modest-size pieces. It may not be true that anything goes, but it is true that many things are worth trying. As the old saying reminds us, rules are made to be broken—a happy thought for those who would rather follow impulses than formulas.

These pages showcase interiors by designers and collectors who, in different ways, met and conquered the challenges of the artful interior. Their solutions range from elegant to eccentric, ultraformal to ultrahip. Some spaces are styled to complement the art, others to contrast with it; but each is successful in its own way, and each tells a story about the art and those who choose to live with it.

One final note: Perfect as they may appear, these interiors are all works in progress. For the dedicated collector, the quest for treasure is an endless adventure, and, happily, no collection is ever really complete.

Modern art doesn't necessarily need a matching environment; it can sometimes flourish best in precisely the opposite. In the foyer of a grand Manhattan town house designed by Nancy Braithwaite, the high-profile presence of an almost-wall-to-wall painting by Atlanta artist Todd Murphy brings a fresh, contemporary edge to the otherwise traditional setting. Architectural moldings, a geometric-patterned stone-and-marble floor, and substantial Biedermeier chairs and stools hold their own against the intensity of the artwork.

To create a background for their museum-caliber collection of early modern furniture and objects, architect-owners Thomas Phifer and Jean Parker Phifer pulled down walls to create a flowing, loftlike feeling in the entry foyer and living room of their high-ceilinged New York apartment. Partial dividers and stepped-up levels helped create a sequence of gallery-like vignettes that set off large-scale graphics by contemporary artists like Sol LeWitt and Brice Marden. Looking toward the entry from the dining area, left, the spare simplicity of the early-twentieth-century bentwood furniture is warmed up by Caio Fonseca's brilliant-colored oil and the sculptural accent of a Gaudi chair. In the living area, above, the bold black of Wiener Werkstätte and Mies van der Rohe furnishings are anchored by a black-and-white geometric rug, perfect foils for the citrus-sharp background of a Frank Stella graphic, the only touch of color in the room.

Myriad graphics and masterful tablescapes reflect the impeccable taste of Boston framer Roger Lussier, whose meticulously planned living room, opposite, houses a varied collection of drawings in an equally diverse mix of frames. The seemingly random arrangement of unrelated works is pulled together by identical cream-colored mats and a surround of shimmering pale tones that keeps the artwork at center stage. Everywhere the eye rests, there is something to delight, with vignettes of sculptures and objects clustered in a play of shapes and textures. In a corner of the room, above left, drawings in unmatched frames are arranged for cozy effect. The parade of miniature drawings over the mantel, in ultrawide mats, above right and opposite, spills over onto the wall beyond.

Industrial-age furniture and accessories often look their best around artwork with the same assertive lines and intense neutral colors. In his Manhattan apartment, photographer John Hall deployed a selection of twentieth-century graphics to complement an enviable mix of collectible modernist furnishings. In the living room, opposite, an angled seating arrangement that includes Breuer and Botta chairs is balanced by the geometry of bold graphics—Robert Mangold, Sol LeWitt, and Joel Shapiro framing the doorway, and a gray-on-black Mangold in the dining room beyond—all set off by walls in strong subtle tones. Over a sleek console, above left, an arrangement of modern glassware plays off Richard Serra's black-on-white graphic. Above right, Eames DCM chairs and Isamu Noguchi's 1955 table, sporting a Danish enameled bowl, Vitra miniature chairs, and Greta Grossman's 1955 Anywhere lamp, create a dining nook. On the wall, a punchy photocollage by the owner has the same edgy appeal as the furnishings and the geometric silhouettes of the art.

In the Santa Fe home of a seasoned collector and art patron, designer Joe D'Urso devised a soft background for a collection of paintings that includes works by New Mexico artists as well as Native American and Spanish Colonial pieces. The unlikely blend works beautifully, creating a living space with the soul-pleasing calm of a desert landscape. In the living room, above left, a minimalist Agnes Martin canvas hangs near a Spanish Colonial armoire whose squared-off moldings complement the geometric lines of its neighbor. In a bedroom, below left, a bold Susan Rothenberg painting looks at home over a sturdy Stickley table. The bathroom, opposite, supplies the surprises with a 1958 Calder mobile suspended over the tub.

Photography, having come into its own as an art form, should be framed with as much care as fine painting. For strong black-and-white images, however, less is generally more. Witness the San Francisco apartment of photographer Jock McDonald, whose favorite images are set in crisp white mats and identical narrow black frames, then hung in soldier-straight lines around the perimeter of the kitchen and dining area. Photographs are double-hung over sink and countertop, left, bringing life to a windowless wall. The view from the dining table, below, looks past the serve-through to the line of photographs in the long entrance hall, leading the eye into the main living space.

Surprisingly sophisticated for its down-home location, this neo-Gothic Victorian residence in Louisville, Kentucky, designed by Todd Klein, features a collection of outspoken artworks in a streamlined interior with Art Deco overtones. In the grandly proportioned living room, above, all eyes are drawn to the painting over the sofa. Tall windows frame it dramatically, and industrial Warren McArthur chairs echo its imagery. In the dining room, below, a mélange of framed artworks is layered on a shallow shelf for a lively arrangement that allows for easy revision. In the master bedroom, right, a Lesley Dill photograph incorporates Emily Dickinson couplets, adding a light touch to the refined Art Deco furniture.

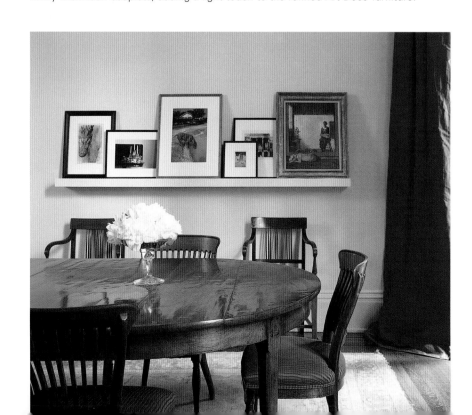

Clearly the home of impassioned collectors, this spacious residence in Tampa, Florida, was designed around the acquisitions of a couple whose enthusiasm for modern art began with their marriage some forty years ago. As newlyweds shopping for furniture on a budget, they bought their first painting— instead of a sofa. When they purchased a vacation home in Florida a few years ago, they called in designer Hal Martin Jacobs to convert the conventional two-story house into an International Style environment to show off some of their most cherished pieces. Jacobs reconfigured the rooms to provide ample breathing space for the sophisticated mix of major paintings, graphics, and sculpture. He gave his clients the all-white environment they expected, but deftly sidestepped stuffiness by a generous use of color and good-humored contrasts. Much of the credit goes to the art itself, a happy family of museum-worthy pieces linked by the common threads of explosive lines and undiluted bright colors. The treasures include prized works by twentieth-century "old masters" Max Beckmann, Jean Dubuffet, and

Strong enough to stand out from any vantage point, a group of Alex Katz portrait lithographs lines up high overhead in the entry hall, right, turning the wall above the flowing stairway into a contemporary frieze. In the formal dining room, above, a modest Miró print leans on a slim glass shelf, set off splendidly by a silver-leaf wall. On the adjacent long wall, Tom Wesselmann's steel cutout nude silhouette has scale enough to suit the space without dominating the room.

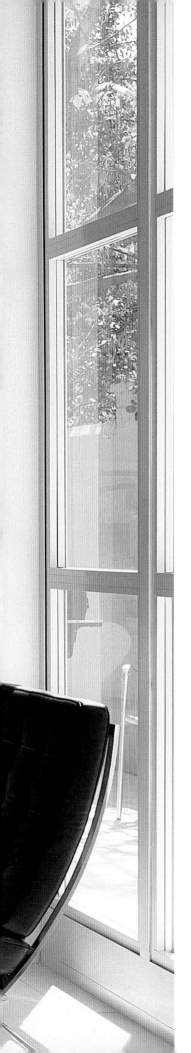

Joan Miró as well as contemporary artists Alex Katz, Jim Dine, and Frank Stella. They're joined by well-chosen architect-designed furniture by the likes of Eero Saarinen and Mies van der Rohe.

With all its name-dropping clout, the collection is more welcoming than intimidating, reflecting both the personalities of the owners and the sunny climate of the locale. The informality that pervades these interiors proves that putting major art in a home needn't mean forsaking a feet-up, casual lifestyle.

Sparking an all-white dining area with exuberant color, left, a suite of Keith Haring prints is massed for architectural presence over an Eero Saarinen Tulip table and Arne Jacobsen Ant chairs. In the foreground is one of a pair of Mies van der Rohe Barcelona chairs, the only nonwhite furniture in the living room. Center stage in the master bedroom, above, Ray Brandt's *Homage to Matisse* screen, inspired by the artist's famed cutouts, is a brilliantly colorful focal point that takes the place of a headboard without detracting from its importance as art.

HOUSE BEAUTIFUL **ART**

74

In the double-height living room, left, furnishings and walls are understated and crisply white, letting the spotlight shine on artworks of brilliance: Jean Dubuffet between the windows, Keith Haring at the left, and a trademark black wood Louise Nevelson sculpture over the fireplace. Smaller objects casually placed throughout underscore the informality of the room despite the richness of the art collection. Above, a suite of Robert Indiana's *Garden of Love* prints stacks up over a Le Corbusier lounge chair.

In a duplex Boston penthouse that might be any
bachelor's fantasy, designer Celeste Cooper fashioned an assertive environment of
mahogany-wrapped walls and geometric lines that sets the stage for a collection of
angular contemporary paintings and strong linear furnishings. The owner, a real
estate developer, built the apartment on top of a converted factory. Having the freedom to create these interiors from scratch gave him the enviable advantage of being
able to design the space specifically to suit his taste and needs and to accommodate
the distinctive art he collects. That translated into customized features such as built-
in banquettes, recessed niches, and display shelves sized to suit particular objects.

The decor is pulled together with sleek surfaces—polished mahogany,
smooth painted walls, and cool marble—and a color palette that leans to dark neutral
tones with occasional jolts of boldness to keep things lively. Sumptuous fabrics with
textural interest such as velvet and glossy leather are used throughout in place of

pattern. The furnishings are straight-
lined but soft-edge midcentury designs
by Jean-Michel Frank and Edward
Wormley, their generous proportions
chosen to complement the art without
lessening its effect.

Contrasts of horizontal and vertical
elements punctuate the black-and-white envelope of the
apartment. At the top of the stairs leading to the second level of
the duplex, opposite, is a bold vertical painting by Mark Luyten.
In the entry-hall alcove, above, a Theodoros Stamos painting is
set into an alcove flanked by lancelike sconces and underscored
by the horizontal lines of a sleek black lacquer console table.

A brilliant red-and-black Stamos painting on the polished-mahogany media wall, above, echoes the straight lines of the fireplace, staircase, and built-in shelves. Proving that even small-scale art can work against a bold background, miniature oriental porcelains, left, line up together on the mantel ledge and in a shadow-box recess above it. In the upstairs bedroom, opposite, a tiny Luyten painting is beefed up with maximum white matting and a strong black frame, then hung off-center over the recessed fireplace. The repeated geometric elements are a consistent theme that ties the elements together and suits the generous scale of the well-conceived space.

House as Canvas

SOME INTERIORS ARE DESIGNED TO BE WORKS OF ART in themselves. In contradiction to the assumption that art consists only of objects that can be hung, mounted, or installed, the walls of these rooms abandon their customary roles as background to become uniquely original creations. Enveloped in fantasies of color or texture, landscape, or faux material, they change the simple act of entering a room into a transporting experience. In these ingeniously conceived spaces, the pleasure of living with art takes on new and enriched meaning.

This idea is hardly a new one. In prehistoric times, indigenous artists painted images on walls, in part as a means of communication but also to enhance the surroundings in which they lived.

The tools for such transformations are often nothing more than paints and brushes, but the execution is far from simple. Skilled artisans turn familiar spaces into fantasies of childhood or visions of exotic lands. A painted ceiling becomes a skyscape of celestial bodies, a muraled entrance foyer recaptures the charm of a country estate, a trompe l'oeil whimsy masks the awkward proportions of a narrow hall, and a row of faux columns brings architectural interest to a boxlike space. Taking a more conservative approach, walls can be stenciled or painted to assume the look of fabric, marble, exotic wood, or stone.

Paints aren't the only raw material for creating an artistic surround. There are as many options offered by paper, textiles, plaster, and, of course, wood and tile, particularly when applied by trained craftspeople—everything from replicating the intricacies of ancient mosaics to the touch-me texture of velvet and tooled leather to the dimensional depth of carved reliefs that create the look of centuries past. Even the most modern spaces can be enhanced by such techniques.

In the bedroom of his New York loft, opposite, artist and designer John D. Oetgen transformed his walls into a gallery of fantasy forms. Seen through the doorway against a backdrop of faux paintings in faux frames is a quirky Michele De Lucchi Memphis-modern chair and a gargantuan pear.

Painted forms in the living room of Oetgen's loft, above, add artistry to the solid walls without becoming intrusive. The shadows are an imaginative touch that double the pattern accent of an openwork iron screen. In the designer's Atlanta home, left, painted pods and spiral shapes evoke the imagery of earth and eternal life on a room-size canvas. Opposite: Oetgen added wit to the formal salon of a client's Manhattan apartment using white acrylic paints on low-gloss soft watercolor blue to weave a Fragonard-like dream of free-form shapes suggesting clouds and flowers.

A whimsical
painted mural devised by Charlotte Moss
turns a pool house into a summery
dining room. The art wraps the walls
in soft colors, swirling forms, and
scattered schools of fish, creating a
delightful impression of an underwater
retreat. The pastel tiled floor and light-
scaled furniture anchor the scheme
without detracting from its airy appeal.

Trompe-l'oeil
carpet, dado-high stencils, and
Pompeiian red upper walls transform
a door-cluttered hallway, opposite,
into a virtual artwork, wittily crowned
with an improvisational mobile. In
the dining room, above right, a pastel
painting defines the palette for
a different take on the dado: a neat
row of oversize dots that encircles
the room and visually pushes out the
walls. In the bedroom, below right,
which has no views, the painted walls
become an agreeable substitute
skyscape that can't be disturbed by
the vagaries of weather.

The eighteenth-century London town house
of decorative painting specialist David Carter is a visual feast of fantasy environments. Almost every surface is part of an expansive canvas that Carter's army of crafts-people has turned into a full-house work of art. The kitchen, right, boasts a geometric painted floor and classical motifs on the walls. Even the garbage bin has a decorative finish. Romantic panels in the powder room, above, contrast with a mural of classical elements in the hallway. In the master bath, below, the Empire tub, floors, and ceiling are painted in exuberant Pompeiian revival style.

In eighteenth-century France, hand-painted wallpapers turned entire rooms into landscapes. In a soigné New York apartment, above, designer Benjamin Noriega-Ortiz spotlighted the museum-quality panels in the dining room with diaphanous silk hangings in the arched doorway that offers a tantalizing glimpse of the sylvan scene beyond. In the classical foyer of a Park Avenue apartment designed by Ann Andrews, right, muralist Robert Jackson devised a wraparound evocation of the Virginia countryside, recalling the former residence of the nostalgic owners.

At first sight nothing seems to resemble Eudoxia less than the design of that carpet. But if you can paused and examine it carefully, you become convinced that each place in the carpet corresponds to a place in the city and all the things contained in the city are included in the design, arranged according to their true relationship, which escapes your eye distracted by the bustle, the throngs, the shoving. All of Eudoxia's confusion, the mules' braying, the lamp ... smell is what is evident in the ind ... you grasp but the carpet pr ... int from which the city shows its ... geometrical scheme implicit i ...

It is easy to get l ... hen you concentrate and s ... u recognize the street you were seeking in a crimson or indigo or magenta thread which, in a wide loop, brings you to the purple enclosure that is your real destination. Every inhabitant of Eudoxia compares the carpet's immobile order with his own image of the city, an anguish of his own, and each can find, concealed among the arabesques, an answer, the story of his life, the twists of fate.

Italo Calvino, *Invisible Cities*, pg. 96

Some of the most extraordinary artists of the mid-twentieth century were those who applied their skills to furniture design. Generally trained as architects, and often practicing design and architecture with equal skill, their chairs in particular are the mainstays of most museum galleries of modern design—and of the collection acquired for and displayed in this rambling New York City apartment. Here works by midcentury American designers join an international gathering of chairs that includes pieces by Swiss, Dutch, Italian, and German masters, from the Bauhaus era to the postmodern generation. They all add up to a congenial mix in a setting with considerable presence and its own quixotic style, a spectacularly colorful residential "design gallery" that is refreshingly un-museumlike. Given the daunting job of pulling it all together, architect Fred Schwartz avoided the convention of modernist white walls in favor of bold colors and attention-getting accents, respectfully

Works from different decades
and countries shake up the straitlaced architecture in the living room, above, with chairs by modern masters Gerrit Rietveld, Frank Lloyd Wright, and Frank Gehry, and an Isamu Noguchi table on a witty rug that abstracts a plan of New York City. The fire screen was designed by Schwartz. In the dining area, opposite, several Robert Venturi chairs join a Mies van der Rohe chair and a Schwartz-designed Skyscraper chair. The quotation screened in a frieze around the room tops off the unusual mix.

deferring to the objects while refusing to be intimidated by them. In another departure from the expected, he declined to restructure the space into a starkly modern environment, leaving the basic framework of the prewar interiors largely intact, from baseboards and cove moldings to paneled doors. Playing off this background, he created a setting that, rather than receding, actually interacts with the objects. The walls are woven into the artistic composition. In the living and dining rooms, excerpts from Italian critic Italo Calvino's *Invisible Cities* are turned into provocative wall graphics, stimulating the intellect as well as the eye; on the foyer

walls, overscale abstract roses recall motifs used by both Charles Rennie Mackintosh and Robert Venturi. The overall result is an apartment that's a virtual paradigm of the individualistic, art-centered home, committed to dynamic pattern and freewheeling improvisation.

The entry hall, opposite, announces the apartment's unconventional approach to museum-caliber modern design, with walls stenciled in an abstract rose motif. The neat lineup of chairs by (left to right) Wright, Mies van der Rohe, Eames, Venturi, and Gehry is a prelude to the treasures beyond. In the sitting room, below left, a tall Bruce Robbins painting establishes the lively color scheme; Marcel Breuer and Gerald Summers chairs and a Murano vase are supporting players. In the bedroom, below right, contemporary leaded-glass panels are a foil for two additional modern classics, a 1957 Eames rocker and a Mies Barcelona table.

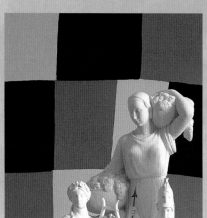

Improvisations

Some interiors are precisely as you would expect them to be. Others are as varied and idiosyncratic as the individuals who inhabit them. Rooms may follow traditional lines, or they may flout convention in the choice of art and the way in which different styles, periods, and media coexist. Being open to both approaches provokes us to look at objects in new ways, to let them challenge, inspire, and broaden the boundaries of our experience.

Redefining Art

WHAT, PRECISELY, DO WE MEAN BY ART? OR BEAUTY? Are aesthetic qualities intrinsic to an object itself, or do they exist only in the response of the viewer? Scholars have debated the question for centuries, but collectors have their own answer: Art, or indeed anything beautiful, is what makes the breath catch, the heart beat, and the pulse quicken. It can be something entirely different for each of us.

Though an art collection once meant only paintings or sculpture, in today's eclectic and inclusive worldview, art objects can be family mementos, travel souvenirs, or objects linked to work and hobbies. They may be carved of wood, woven of fiber, molded of clay, wrought from metal, or assembled from ephemera. The choice is determined by personal taste as much as—or even more than—connoisseurship.

For those with eyes open to perceive it and minds open to appreciate it, art is everywhere. It can be a cabinet filled with vintage lunch boxes or a window-frame arrangement of heraldic medallions; it can be a wall papered with vintage movie posters, a Valentine-variety of Victorian etchings, a suspension of model sailboats. Sometimes, the difference between art and bric-a-brac is not so much what the objects are as how they're displayed. Meticulously mounted and gracefully framed, cosseted in their own cabinetry, or composed into careful tablescapes, personal collections of everyday objects can be as appealing as more conventional and costlier treasures. And since the line dividing art from kitsch is a fine one, and increasingly blurred, what separates the soup can in a cupboard from the object in a Warhol painting is as much a matter of attitude as of substantive difference. Even everyday objects can acquire some of the presence—and give as much of the pleasure—as works universally acknowledged as art.

With a bit of imagination, any number of unexpected objects can be transformed into art. To fill up a plain white wall in the living room of a Connecticut country house, designer T. Keller Donovan cut apart a Paris street map, framed the pieces in thirty matching squares, and hung them in a wall treatment that's long on design impact, short on expense, and strong enough to balance the intensity of the sunflower-yellow upholstery.

Finding pleasure in the most prosaic objects, architect Steven Ehrlich and his wife, Marlo, devised a wall of shelves in the open kitchen of their Santa Monica beach house that instantly transformed a whimsical collection of 1950s lunch boxes into a veritable work of art. Seen at a distance, the painted objects are a kaleidoscope of colors; up close, they're a treasure trove of nostalgic images and cartoon-character humor.

A jewel box of a house in California, built by Charles Eastlake in 1889, is brought up-to-the-minute by designer Stephen Shubel with a funky mixture of old and not-quite-new. In the living room, left, a Vilma Banky flapper-era theatrical poster is a perfect partner for a squashy sofa in down-to-earth denim. The setting, capped off with period sconces and a quirky modern light, is refreshingly unpompous. In another interior, above, a vintage French advertising poster takes on artistic airs in a cozy corner. It teams up with a Victorian birdcage and winsome wicker furniture; for added impact, the accent colors are keyed to the poster.

Treating anonymous folk art and vernacular furnishings with the same respect as old masters, designers Peter Ermacora and Evan Hughes dressed a classic nineteenth-century New England country house in Americana style to show off their favorite objects. The mix of country-cabinetmaker furnishings in charmingly unmatched arrangements suits the rural environment and keeps the objects in focus. In the entrance hall, above, nineteenth-century horse-shaped copper weather vanes flank the front door, and cast-iron deer antlers make a complementary table base. The inviting seating arrangement in the living room, below, is kept off-balance with accents like a Chinese armchair, a spool-legged needlepoint stool, and unmatched tables. William Morris wallpaper wraps the bedroom, opposite, in pattern, setting off the slim-lined pencil-post bed and vernacular country chairs. A nineteenth-century hooked rug hangs on the wall like a prized painting, and a folk-art dog plays sentinel at the foot of the bed.

Ingenious use of color is an art in itself. In the small living room of T. Keller Donovan's New York apartment, above left, red and white add firecracker verve that seems to magnify the space. Making much of a small-scale, colorful collection of heraldic engravings, he bordered them with crisp white mats and lipstick-red frames, while reversed-color framing sparks the graphics in the hallway beyond. In another city brownstone living room, below left, a close-knit sextet of celestial maps adds blue-and-white bull's-eyes of color to wake up a stodgy Victorian mantel. Opposite, more proof that everyday objects can be given artistic license: Designer Jeffrey Bilhuber turned an assortment of antique wax seals into an eye-catching framed focal point on the wall of a Pennsylvania farmhouse. In front of it is a nineteenth-century papier-mâché chair.

Making objets d'art from flea-market finds that less keen eyes might overlook, designer Adam Dolle gave his New York apartment a stylish funkiness that suits its downtown neighborhood, as well as a highly individualistic view of what constitutes art. Against chocolate walls in the master bedroom, above left and right, bits and pieces of graphics and ephemera are neatened up and hung in crisp, narrow frames. A stream-of-consciousness assortment of photos and newspaper clippings are mounted on wood-framed kraft-paper bulletin boards. In the mantel recess, opposite, is an assemblage of an Op art–like string construction dating to the 1970s, a Belgian vase, and a three-dimensional New Zealand wire sculpture.

A lifelong admirer of seafaring despite the mostly landlubber life he lives in urban Atlanta, designer and antiques dealer Toby West exercised his fantasy in the distinctly personal collection of nautical objects he acquired for his Florida vacation home. In the charmingly retro community of Seaside, the house is new, but it has the old-fashioned look of a sailing captain's cottage. Doing a switch on the usual collector's story, West acquired the house before the objects, then decided to decorate it to suit the location. He chose boats and sailing as a theme that would both flatter the interiors and bring the sea indoors.

To set the mood, he added a stair banister reminiscent of a rooftop admiral's walk and punched porthole windows in several of the walls. Then he fitted out the rooms in seaworthy style with objects that any seaman would covet, turning the house into a virtual naval museum.

On the wall of the library, opposite, narrow wooden shelves show off a collection of ships in bottles and a miscellany of nautical instruments against a background wallpapered with antique Coast Guard maps. On the game table is a rare four-armed nineteenth-century tramp art candelabra, and on the wall a porthole window and nautical images. The geometric imagery of a nineteenth-century Southern folk-art mantel, above, is a stabilizing anchor for the mix of objects and pictures. An English sailing ship diorama completes the vignette.

His fascinating assortment of rarities ranges from maps and sailing-ship dioramas to ship models and seamasters' instruments, most of them acquired during his frequent business trips to England. He installed them throughout the house in arrangements that treat the objects as seriously as conventional art. Eschewing the obvious sea-blue palette in favor of a mix of sailor-white and no-color neutrals, he finished the spit-and-polish interiors with mostly nineteenth-century pieces, making copious use of white canvas upholstery. The combination results in an inviting and comfortable interior, even in the face of such a dominant and highly specialized theme—so much so that when the house was recently sold, the buyer, though not a collector, insisted on taking it with every object intact.

The main attraction in the dining room, left, is a wall-mounted display of West's collection of "pond yachts," prized possessions of Victorian Englishmen who sailed them in public parks. In the kitchen, above left, an English oak dresser base with a hanging shelf holds carved sandpipers and an American platter-and-plate set. The stairwell walls, above right, are filled with 1800s woolworks and dioramas, objects crafted by wives while their husbands were away at sea. The brass chandelier and crucifix are French accents.

Contrast and Counterpoint

ART MAY BE DEMANDING, BUT IT DOESN'T NECESSARILY demand surroundings to match. Treating it seriously needn't mean approaching it on tiptoe, or throwing freedom of expression out the window. In creating an artful interior, taking liberties is not only permissible, it's often preferable to treading a more familiar path. Of course, it's perfectly appropriate to coordinate: modern with modern, traditional with traditional, minimal or oversize objects or artwork in the same media arranged together. On the other hand, the assumption that only similar objects or styles are compatible can restrict the imagination. A more venturesome approach may show that opposites not only attract but can be the best of companions.

A traditional interior, for example, has much to gain from the addition of modern art, which can serve as a counterpoint to the architectural framework and the weightiness of the furnishings. And a self-consciously modern interior might be softened by striking a balance between old and new in sculpture and paintings. The "mix" approach can take many directions: assembling disparate objects in one interior, pitting one style of furnishings against a contrasting style of art, playing art off architecture, or intensifying the experience of color by an occasional clash. An eclectic mix of interiors and objects often makes the most interesting interior in which to live. And such a home is apt to seem the result of serendipity rather than the product of painstaking design.

How to put it all together? By keeping an open mind. Although there are a number of possible wrongs—too much to fit the space, too heavy to hang on the walls, too cluttered to allow access through a room—there is no single right. One of the keys is to trust your own taste, your own judgment, your own ability to know what kind of surroundings make you most comfortable.

Unlikely companions: Folk art and fine art pair up starkly and stylishly in a modern hallway in Santa Fe. Designer Joe D'Urso teamed the clean, geometric lines of the painting and the rough-textured finish of the Spanish Colonial chest to set the tone for the art-filled minimalist home beyond.

The densely furnished living room of designer Eric Cohler's Manhattan town house apartment, above, is a kaleidoscope of styles. An irresistible clutter of unrelated collections, the fruit of extensive travel, invades every corner in English-country-house fashion. Yet the unlikely combinations work beautifully as a whole. Helping to achieve this is the surround of intense color and a single bold pattern on upholstery that anchors a magpie-mix of cultures and media, including objects as diverse as Chinese porcelains, African carvings, and contemporary photographs. Over Chinese-red walls, opposite, the high ceiling is painted to appear even higher, with a fanciful night sky in deep blues, gold-leaf stars, even a man in the moon.

Spare and striking, black and white, old and new are juxtaposed in the foyer of a modern California home. Floating narrow shelves, arranged with deceptive casualness by architect Paul Rudolph, create a showcase for African sculpture and contemporary photography. Contrasting strong vertical and horizontal elements make a dramatic welcome to the house.

At home in a seventeenth-century Dutch castle, photographer René Stoeltie and his wife, Barbara, have sparingly arranged classical sculpture and furnishings in a series of airy, whitewashed spaces for a surprisingly modern look. Against a paneled wall, opposite, part of a collection of nineteenth-century bisque figurines from Sèvres, Copenhagen, and Niderviller stands out in sharp relief against an abstract geometric painting. Above right, an imposing gesso sculpture representing the Hermes of the Capitoline, its size belied by the grand space, sits on an architectural platform. Pale Gustavian colors on the upholstered pieces—a 1940s chaise and Neoclassical chairs—soften the crisp white background and the black-and-white artworks. The lighthearted question-mark form of Maroeska Metz's massive curly metal sculpture, below right, introduces the twentieth century into the beautifully detailed drawing room, already home to a nineteenth-century parian bust and Russian chair.

For his southern California home, architect Stephen Harby designed a living room centered on a cozy, cushioned inglenook inspired by early German modernist architect Peter Behrens's own house in Darmstadt. A frieze of Asian folk-art masks, opposite—a striking graphic composition in its own right— wraps around the entablature of the room; its square panels repeat the geometry of the windows and the fireplace surround. A palette of intense colors helps to organize the mix of folk-art objects and the owner's own architectural watercolors. On an iron-based table, above, a menagerie of elephant figures offers a visually appealing contrast of materials, sizes, and colors.

Occasionally, a successful interior is not only the result of a planned convergence of styles but also the product of chance. This house is one such example. Its peripatetic owner is a tireless collector, a successful executive who develops creative imagery for high-profile corporate clients. He has built homes in different parts of the country, a different art-saturated atmosphere in each. Several years ago, after straying from his youthful devotion to classic mod-ernism, he unexpectedly returned to those roots. He purchased a 1965 Richard Neutra-inspired International Style house in Scottsdale, Arizona, then called on architect John Chonka to update the design for contemporary living.

Chonka totally reconfigured the house. On the ground floor, a

In the entry hallway, opposite, a portrait of Oskar Kokoschka hangs in spare splendor on a straw-colored wall. A seventeenth-century reliquary on a Spanish refectory table anchors a mélange of objects. In the dining room, above, warm wood backgrounds and a honed stone floor set the stage for a blend of styles, shapes, and periods. The precise composition of objects on the white mahogany sideboard includes African masks, a large wooden mortar and pestle, and native pottery; a seventeenth-century Italian portrait hangs above it. Dining is on sleek Mario Bellini Cab chairs around an extravagantly grained bleached rosewood conference table.

series of spacious rooms forms a U around an atrium patio; a yellow-tiled stairway leads to more private quarters above. The original all-white interiors were transformed with warmer neutrals and bursts of pure primary color. On a whim, the owner then shipped a handful of his long-owned contemporary art collection from his New York apartment "just to see how they looked," expecting to acquire art more suited to the laid-back locale. Instead, the new environment revived the art and gave him a new sense of excitement about what he already owned.

Today, important modernist works coexist with fine examples of regional art without succumbing to either a strict doctrine of International Style or the faux-Spanish ambience of many interiors in this part of the country. The house is furnished with a mix that includes midcentury modern pieces, Conquistador-era objects in Spanish Colonial style, and the occasional surprise of a locally crafted piece. The blend is a fine complement to the art collection, which has been broadened to cross international and cultural boundaries in an emphatic and highly personal mix. In both art and furnishings, the polished and the primitive set up a play of opposites that brings out the most attractive features of both.

Still engaged in collecting, in a variety of different disciplines, the homeowner has learned that good pieces can shine anywhere, even in places where they might have seemed inappropriate. He now enjoys the stimulation of seeing his collections in different surroundings, often moving them around from place to place and even from house to house.

Playing off the familiar modernist open-to-the-landscape living room, twentieth-century furnishings combine with tribal artifacts. Over the fireplace is a painting by Picasso student Antonio Giliolli. Silhouetted against one window is an imposing Oceanic shield; in the other is an African antelope sculpture. In the front corner of the room is a sculpture by Tucson artist Thomas Filabaum, an abstract crayon-marked human form that represents a Native American chief.

White mahogany walls in the library, opposite, are a flattering backdrop for another, more subtle play of contrasts: a horizontal parade of framed drawings, including four Elie Nadelman works and an Albrecht Dürer, and several small sculptures. Above them, the circular form of a Robert Dash painting is flanked by chock-full-of-art-book built-in shelves, themselves a testament to the owner's passion. The warmed-up neutral scheme carries into the adjoining master bedroom, below, where paneled walls frame the bed alcove. The figural form in a surrealistic Gerd Bonfert photograph seems to be echoed by a wood folk figure from the Nicobar Islands. A witty Peter Shire wood sculpture and a Japanese *tansu* chest span a continuum of shape, scale, and century.

The New York City apartment designed by

Frédéric Méchiche houses a choice collection of spirited contemporary painting and sculpture focused on assertive, abstractionist artworks. One would generally expect to see such pieces in starkly modern surroundings filled with straight-lined modern furniture, but visitors here are more likely to be delighted than disconcerted. Instead of the Bauhaus aesthetic, these interiors more closely resemble those of an eighteenth-century country house. Given the raw material of highbeamed, well-proportioned rooms, Méchiche made the most of the setting by leaving well enough alone—for the most part. He did add subtle Palladian arches on doorways and a space-expanding mirrored niche in the entry to enhance the existing features without intruding on them. Then, to avoid the distraction of intense color, he chose a simple yet sophisticated palette—gentle taupe and celadon for the walls, pale sisal for the floors, and crisp black-and-white fabrics on the shapely Neoclassical upholstered pieces. He kept the

In the library/dining room, above, a Joaquin Torres-Garcia abstract painting holds its own in a sea of classical furniture. Between molding-detailed bookcases on one wall of the same room, opposite, a dramatic black-on-black James Brown painting forms a backdrop for a curvy Regency-reproduction settee. Stopping short of the cove molding, the bookcases accentuate the ceiling's height and provide convenient perches for a pair of African animal sculptures.

monotony of too much repeated pattern at bay by covering the armchairs with medium-slim stripes and using skinny ones on the gilded pieces. Save for the black-and-white marble floor in the foyer, the absence of bold pattern helps keep attention on the art.

That art appears not to be arranged, but in fact is placed in strategic open spaces, mingling with the furniture in graceful groupings that encourage a flow of movement from one room to another. Deliberately unmatched, the furnishings are light in scale and set at angles to offset the formality of their classical silhouettes. The result is a focused, calm, cleverly choreographed, and eminently successful marriage of supposed opposites.

An unframed oil on canvas by Jean Charles Blais in the dining room, opposite, mixes it up with an Early American dining table and Regency-style chairs. In the living room, below, black-and white paintings on either side of the archway from the dining room play visual Ping-Pong with the stripes on the upholstered and open arm chairs.

On the window wall of the living room,
right, a tiny but vivid Andy Warhol flower painting in a shadow-box frame (detail above) hangs over the Egyptian frieze of a Gustavian sofa. On the coffee table, a clutch of red poppies repeats the painting's colors (detail below). With a one-note color scheme like this, a bit of contrasting color makes the difference between pleasant and perfect.

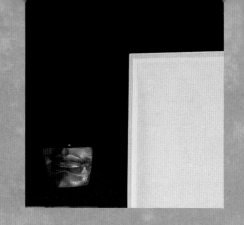

Presenta

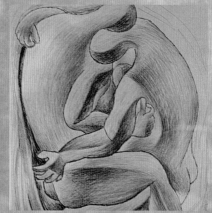

Making art the focus of a home involves more than just deciding where to place the artworks. It means working with the house's existing architecture and with its furniture, whose primary objective is comfort. And it means making choices of background, color, framing, lighting, and display, all of which affect the way in which works of art are perceived and enjoyed. In the artful home, ease of living meets gallery showcase with stunning results.

The Right Backdrop

As a fine gem needs the proper setting, so do objects of art. Living with art involves deciding not just what to own but how to set it off—establishing a stage on which the art can star without upstaging the supporting players.

The scale of the space, the dimensions of the rooms, the location of walls, stairs, and doorways, the orientation of the interiors toward natural light—these are a home's architectural elements. Using them to best advantage to show off art requires a good helping of artful design. At the least, it calls for well-planned placement of objects, from furniture to accessories to the art itself; at most, it demands the reconfiguring of space.

Furniture, and its arrangement, should be chosen for comfort and function as well as for aesthetic appeal, but it doesn't have to "match" the period or style of the art with which it will be sharing space. The only "rule" is that the elements end up in some kind of harmony of scale and proportion.

Next come decisions of color. It was once considered sacrilege to hang paintings on anything but plain white walls, but that's no longer the case. Today's home may be well dressed in coats of many different hues, textures, and materials—painted or paneled, fabric-covered, or even mirrored. In most cases, walls in muted neutrals tend to bring the art into sharper focus. Crayon-box colors, on the other hand, can bring out the tones in a painting or set off the day-and-night contrasts in photographs or etchings. Depending on the choice of surfacing, backgrounds can be deliberately severe or conscientiously inviting; slick surfaces add drama to back up strong objects, gossamer fabrics or velvety wall coverings can soften the linearity of modern works or diffuse reflective surfaces. There's a wealth of materials and color options available today to create the ideal background for every collection, no matter its size or subject.

Paris blues: Playing off the backdrop of a brushstroke-painted blue wall in a Parisian town house, designer Christian Liaigre shows both boldness and restraint in a console-table composition. The assertive background lends cohesiveness to the unusual group of objects, which include an attenuated metal lamp of his own design, a framed graphic, and a classical head.

A subtle-toned background sets off the fine lines of Directoire furniture and a choice selection of art in the studiously uncluttered living room of fashion designer Michael Leva's New York apartment, above. A pair of white Roni Horn paintings is a focal point above the black-upholstered sofa. Taking the reverse tack, opposite, a macho-but-mellow living room gets high-key dramatic effect from smoky-black walls and strong-lined white objects. On a slender shelf, designer Jeffrey Bilhuber arranged a layered lineup of mostly white pieces of art. He completed the non-competitive furnishings with a serene mix of comfortable seating, soft carpeting, and African accents.

In a grand salon

in Manhattan, opposite, designer Pauline Boardman combined different-quality paintings on a soft yellow wall. The color is warmer than white but doesn't compete with, or fight, the art. In his own living room, above, New York designer Robert Couturier made a commitment to vivid color—a ravishing red—to pull together an unabashedly eclectic mix of furniture and artworks. The resulting richness suggests a luscious blend of penthouse and palazzo. Right: In the parlor of a restored 170-year-old house in Georgia, designer Miles Whitfield took a nineteenth-century approach with symmetrical arrangements of art and accessories against acid-green walls. Regency-style furnishings, upholstered in striking black moiré, update the classical look.

A series of intricately detailed hand-painted *japonais* panels, conceived with great originality by designer Greg Jordan and executed with extraordinary skill by Charles R. Gracie & Sons, covers the walls of this luxurious living room. Behind a Condoy chalk-and-pastel drawing, opposite, is one of the panels, mounted on paper and framed in borders stenciled with chinoiserie motifs. The treatment creates a unifying background for a room filled with fine French furnishings spiced with Asian accents and a mix of contemporary art and objects in which almost nothing is precisely the same period or style. On one side of the room, above left, a large graphic by Karim Noureldin is at home with mostly French furnishings and a fine 1860s Tabriz carpet that echoes the warm tones of the room. On the opposite wall, below left, a mixed-media work by Rafael Pimentel and Mike Nolan hangs over the fireplace, and a Richard Serra etching hangs to its right. As an added bonus, the panels are removable.

When wall space is scarce, unexpected backgrounds can be
called into service as staging areas for framed art. In designer Ann Dupuy's New Orleans living
room, opposite, a scene-stealing nude by Robert Gordy holds court in the center of the
triple window, looking into the room at a beige-and-sand-toned landscape of furnishings. The
white John Dickinson animal-leg table is a 1970s rarity. In the New York bedroom of T. Keller
Donovan's space-shy apartment, below, filled-to-bursting bookshelves make an unbroken
backdrop for a quartet of architectural prints illustrating elements of famous American buildings.
Suspended on nearly invisible wires, the pictures can be moved easily for access to books.

Larger-than-life art equals superpower importance. A floor-to-ceiling, wall-to-wall vintage poster accents the drama of a two-story space in Steven and Marlo Ehrlich's California beach house, left. The pool-hall motif takes to a casual arrangement of furniture and an outdoor-size tree in the dining area. In the tiny bedroom of Argentine designer Roberto Bergero, above, the saturated color of a hand-painted wall-size tulip on a raspberry sisal mat makes for an unconventional artwork—and a wittily original headboard.

The artlessly artful fashion sense of celebrated designer Geoffrey Beene shows in every room of his striking Hawaii vacation home. Purchased several years ago, the beachfront house had been built as a site for corporate meetings. Each of the three floors was a separate unit, complete with its own kitchen, and the entire house had been done in shades of pink. For Beene, there was no hesitation: He opened up the space, widened the windows, and installed his favorite color scheme of crisp black and white, adding touches of green to defuse what could have become an overly urban air. The designer's trademark stripes have considerable panache in an informal setting that suits the tropical locale. This combination is both starting point and background for a compelling mix of art, native crafts, and offbeat accents, assembled in a city-slick environment that uses mirrored walls as hanging space. The mirrors work their space-stretching magic in the modest-size rooms and create reflecting images that frame the art in color. The look is pleasantly laid-back but silkily refined.

Crisply tailored black borders define the entry stairs, above; an 1840s Chinese vase framed in the opening between the levels adds a burst of color. Against a mirrored wall in the dining room, opposite, patterns play on an ebony-and-pearl Indian mirror hung over an old kitchen cabinet, found at an auction and newly painted with horizontal stripes. The lamps were made from old gasoline cans.

A painting in gold and burnished tones by a native Hawaiian artist on a mirrored wall, left, establishes a surprisingly flattering backdrop for Wiener Werkstätte modernist chairs and a silver-leaf table. A vintage Deco cabinet, striped in Beene colors, is the underpinning for a bronze nude and a Swedish glass bowl. In the master bedroom, above, a mirror serves as a background for a wall of framed photographs and Pavel Tschelitchew sketches. In a small downstairs bedroom, below, the vertical black-and-white stripes of the contact paper on the walls meet the horizontal ones of the bedspread, a jazzy background for the clean-framed artwork depicting sports figures.

The Art of Display

DESIGNING INTERIORS TO HOUSE ART DOESN'T MEAN turning a home into a museum. It does require the deft use of display: making fine objects look their best, and lesser ones seem more than they are. It doesn't take genius, just a good eye and a few basic guidelines.

With some objects, the choice of placement has an air of inevitability—yes, that's exactly where it belongs. For others, almost any wall or shelf or corner will provide a comfortable perch. The trial-and-error system works well here; if one location doesn't look good, try another.

A great work of art, no matter how modest in size, deserves to be presented solo; most others can be arranged in groups. Objects of the same type or those with similar subject matter, shape, or coloration make the best partners, but dissimilar ones can provide intriguing juxtapositions. Some clutter is appealing; utter confusion is a mistake. Happily, no arrangement is set in stone: The simple regrouping of a tablescape or the transfer of framed drawings from one wall to another can wake up a tired room or show a new side of a familiar object.

The wall—or mirror or window or bookcase—on which a picture hangs, the shelf on which it rests, the height above floor or furniture, the objects or the empty space around it are all important considerations. But for paintings, works on paper, or precious textile fragments, the frame is the primary one. It should be chosen to suit the work, rather than to match the decor (though it's wise to give the setting some thought, to avoid obvious anachronisms of style). Antique frames, themselves rare and collectible, evoke the richness of past centuries to flatter works with the patina of age. For more contemporary art, sleek machine-age materials and forms work well.

Mats—the visual separation between frame and art—can do a lot to enhance a piece of art. Wide ones can beef up a tiny graphic or etching, helping it stand up to weightier neighbors. Though pale mats are the norm,

A serious artwork is given serious treatment: Designer Bunny Williams put a Gilded Age portrait on a real artist's easel and gave it prime position in a double-height living room. There it resides in the stylish company of bold contemporary wall art and a frivolous gilt table.

Properly presented, almost any type of object can stand in for actual pieces of art. Making much from almost nothing, Geoffrey Beene made a hall console by topping a darkroom developing sink with slate, above, then added artful lamps made from the base of a steel birdbath. Opposite, budget-minded designers Reusser Bergstrom Associates used hardware-store molding to panel the walls of a Pasadena living room and set off a collection of African masks.

lively colored ones can turn a cluster of less rarefied treasures into a striking wall arrangement.

As alternatives to nails or picture hooks, paintings can be hung on specially designed systems of horizontal and vertical rods secured to ceiling moldings or suspended on almost-invisible wires or romantic ribbons. Recessed niches and shelves add architectural interest while providing display space. Mantels, shelves, tabletops, pedestals, and platforms make excellent spots for three-dimensional objects; massed, stacked, or clustered, they can be changed around with every new addition.

Lighting is the most critical, and most often neglected, element in display, and the one most fraught with possibilities for error. The nature, scale, and fragility of the art, the amount of available natural light, and the activities for which each room is to be used all play a part in determining the best lighting options. Each type—natural, incandescent, fluorescent, halogen, or fiber-optic—has particular qualities and appropriate use. Such complex choices are best left to experts—who are well worth the added cost.

A strategic mix of miscellany in designer Adam Dolle's New York apartment, opposite, puts an oddball collection of ceramics against a patchwork-painted background that squares off the clutter of odd shapes and sizes. Neatly aligned against another wall, a cluster of framed prints backs up an atomic-era sculpture. In a graceful but narrow foyer designed by Dan Carithers, right, a classical archway frames a plaster sculpture set dramatically on a pedestal that could have come straight from a Grecian ruin.

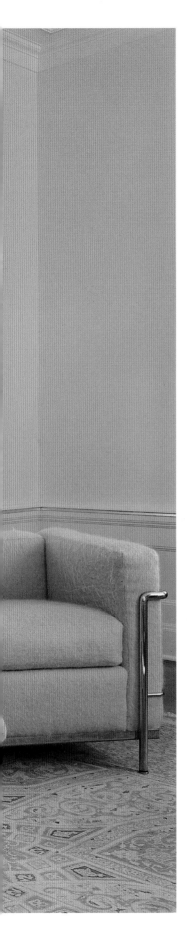

To avoid damaging the interior of a serene contemporary living room, left, designers Stuart Schepps and Audrey Leigh Nevins hung the framed art in front of the walls instead of on them. In her Manhattan apartment, above and below, designer Eve Robinson relied on vertical rods that float the art away from the walls. Each picture is mounted on a rod by means of clips fastened to the back of its frame; the clips move up or down to fit the size of the frame they must accommodate. The verticals are then suspended from molding-high horizontal rods mounted into the wall.

Three framed photographs over the mantel of a Paris living room, opposite, are offset, and balanced, by the attenuated lines of two Christian Liaigre lamps. In the dining area, above, closely hung portraits by photographer Patrick Faigenbaum have the visual weight of a single dramatic work. Liaigre designed the treatment, as well as the chairs and keg-shape table, whose spare lines and palpable textures speak of both the ancient and the avant-garde.

Smaller pieces of art can be lost when left to fend for themselves. But when they're put in similar frames and grouped together, they can make a memorable statement. A collection of English Regency cutouts, opposite, surrounds a pair of nineteenth-century watercolors mounted over a miniature tablescape in a Los Angeles home. The total effect is a charming riff on British-country-house style. In a dining room by designer Suzanne Rheinstein, above, scores of bird watercolors from an eighteenth-century folio, framed in wavy glass to suit the period, line up on painted and glazed striped walls. Tiny prints floating in oversize mats, right, are arranged, ziggurat-style, in a corner of designer Thomas Pheasant's Georgetown cottage.

An elegant Palladian villa in Portugal gave designer David Hicks plenty of room for design artistry, right down to the precise, uncluttered tablescapes on almost every surface. Above left, a swirling abstract painting is balanced by neatly paired accessories on the geometric cabinet beneath. Above right, a casual arrangement of framed graphics takes well to a floral garnish. Opposite: Proving that artful talents often run in families, a graceful tablescape in the London home of Ashley and Allegra Hicks, David Hicks's son and daughter-in-law, shows how a designing couple's different tastes converge in offbeat contrasts. The objects include a 1928 Cecil Beaton photograph, a modern drawing by Donald Baechler, and a cast of the nose of Michelangelo's David on a copper-base console designed by Allegra Hicks.

For one of the country's leading interior designers,

Vicente Wolf lives in surprisingly simple style. The spacious New York loft he calls home is remarkably informal and undecorated—or so it seems at first glance. On closer examination, however, it's clear that the appeal of the space is the work of a masterful hand and that the loft's casual urbanity is precisely the goal he had in mind.

An interior and furniture designer, compulsive traveler, and skilled amateur photographer, Wolf had an enviable framework in which to weave his spell: a light-flooded, expansive space with industrial-size windows that encompass wide-angle vistas of downtown Manhattan and the Hudson River. In these surroundings he devised a highly personal aerie, first wrapping the entire space in his favorite envelope of white walls and floor. Against this forgiving background, eccentric pairings of artworks and mementos from his travels mingle the funky with the fabulous. After many years, his sharp eye has built a collection that crosses countries and time periods. Its display within the loft is equally diverse. Everywhere the eye goes are intriguing objects, placed apparently at random, but in truth arranged with careful precision.

A tranquil Thai buddha, above, sits on a 1940s French pool chaise, unflustered by its association with Robert Mapplethorpe and Diane Arbus photographs. Framed photographs, opposite, are hung on walls or propped on easels, anchoring an informal arrangement of furniture that includes a gilded Louis XVI bench.

Wolf's skill at arrangement is evident throughout—in the sweep of space, in the use of multiple levels and surfaces for display, and in the sheer diversity of artworks that inhabit the same space without striking a single discordant note. Rather than attempting to force the collection to appear to be a single unit, he mixed it up with groupings of his own black-and-white photographs. The crisp geometry of the prints, in their white mats and minimal black frames, plays off the exotic objects. A spare selection of mostly white-upholstered furniture studiously avoids competition with the art treasures.

Sporting different frames, but all in black, the designer's photographs, above left, wrap around the walls at lower-than-usual height, leading the eye directly to the spectacular window views. Wolf's eclectic choice of furniture makes for surprising juxtapositions, such as a 1950s desk with a nailhead-trimmed French chair, above right. In the bedroom, opposite, a curvy, white-covered *bateau en lit* nestles against the windows, where still more photos lean against the sill to avoid blocking the view and unframed blowups landscape the walls. Save for the blue of the sky outside, or the golden artificial evening light, there is virtually no color in the space. With such other pleasures for the eye, it isn't missed.

Directory of Designers and Architects

DD Allen & Michael Pierce
Pierce Allen
New York, NY
(212) 627-5440

James Aman & Anne Carson
Aman & Carson, Inc.
New York, NY
(212) 794-8878

Ann Andrews Interiors
Washington, DC
(202) 244-4233

Piero Castellini Baldissera
Milan, Italy
011-39-02-4800-5384

Roberto Bergero
Paris, France
011-33-142-72-0351

Jeffrey Bilhuber
New York, NY
(212) 308-4888

Pauline Boardman, Ltd.
New York, NY
(212) 288-8379

Nancy Braithwaite Interiors
Atlanta, GA
(404) 355-1740

Dan Carithers Design Consultant
Atlanta, GA
(404) 355-8661

David Carter Interior Design
London, England
011-44-207-790-0259

John Chonka
True Order Architects
Phoenix, AZ
(602) 256-2345

Eric Cohler Incorporated
New York, NY
(212) 737-8600

Celeste Cooper
Repertoire
New York, NY
(212) 826-5667

Robert Couturier, Inc.
New York, NY
(212) 463-7177

Adam Dolle, Inc.
New York, NY
(212) 541-7006

T. Keller Donovan, Inc.
New York, NY
(212) 760-0537

Ann Dupuy
Holden & Dupuy
New Orleans, LA
(504) 897-1100

Joe D'Urso
D'Urso Design, Inc.
East Hampton, NY
(631) 329-3634

Steven Ehrlich Architects
Culver City, CA
(310) 838-9700

**Peter Ermacora &
Evan G. Hughes**
E.G.H. Peter, Inc.
Norfolk, CT
(860) 542-5221

Michelle Halard
Paris, France
011-33-144-07-1400

Stephen Harby
Santa Monica, CA
(310) 450-8239

Ashley & Allegra Hicks
Allegra Hicks Design
London, England
011-44-207-351-9696

Robert Jackson
Germantown, NY
(518) 828-1805

**Hal Martin Jacobs &
Associates**
New York, NY
(212) 355-1207

Greg Jordan, Inc.
New York, NY
(212) 570-4470

Carole Katleman Interiors
Beverly Hills, CA
(310) 248-2464

Todd Klein, Inc.
New York, NY
(212) 414-0001

David Lake
Lake/Flato Architects, Inc.
San Antonio, TX
(210) 227-3335

Christian Liaigre
Paris, France
011-33-1-5363-3366

Roger Lussier, Inc.
Boston, MA
(617) 536-0069

Ned Marshall, Inc.
New York, NY
(212) 879-3672

Frédéric Méchiche
Paris, France
011-33-1-4278-7828

Charlotte Moss
Easton-Moss & Co.
New York, NY
(212) 772-6244

Benjamin Noriega-Ortiz
New York, NY
(212) 343-9709

John D. Oetgen
Oetgen Design, Inc.
Atlanta, GA
(404) 352-1112

Gaetano Pesce
Pesce, Ltd.
New York, NY
(212) 941-0280

Thomas Pheasant, Inc.
Washington, DC
(202) 337-6596

Thomas Phifer & Jean Parker Phifer
Thomas Phifer & Partners
New York, NY
(212) 337-0334

Reusser-Bergstrom Associates
Pasadena, CA
(626) 441-6761

Suzanne Rheinstein & Associates
West Hollywood, CA
(310) 550-8900

Eve Robinson Associates
New York, NY
(212) 595-0661

Stuart Schepps & Audrey Leigh Nevins
DSGN Interior Design Inc.
Cedar Grove, NJ
(973) 857-7722

Frederic Schwartz
Schwartz Architects
New York, NY
(212) 741-3021

Stephen Shubel Design
Ross, CA
(415) 925-9332

Toby West Limited
Atlanta, GA
(404) 233-7425

Miles Gandy Whitfield
Charleston, SC
(843) 971-4376

Bunny Williams, Inc.
New York, NY
(212) 207-4040

Vicente Wolf Associates
New York, NY
(212) 465-0590

Photography Credits

The room on the front jacket was designed by DD Allen
and Michael Pierce; page 1, Carole Katleman;
page 2, DD Allen and Michael Pierce; page 5, Ned
Marshall; pages 6–7, James Aman and Anne Carson;
page 8, Eve Robinson; page 173, Frédéric Méchiche; page
174, Adam Dolle; page 176, John D. Oetgen.